Crossing Rivers

Poems of the sayings of the Buddha

Kelly Fields

Catherine Fields - editor

Diana Cojocaru – cover art

kelthscreations.blog

Preface

I wrote these poems after listening to the Sayings of the Buddha. It took over a year to write them, and six months to compile the book. I wrote them from an interpretation of the Dhammapada. My goal was to gain a greater knowledge of the way that the Buddha taught of. Maybe with this being in a more modern poem form it will inspire us to follow the path of all the great Masters and one day we will awake to find the true Master inside our hearts.

Namaste

The Robe

If thoughts are led by an impure mind, then only sorrow you will find.

Your mind is pure and will be known, as a happy being this will be shown.

Become a victim of your mind in life, it will embrace hatred and strife.

Forgive the wrongs done to you, your mind will tell hatred to shoo.

Use hatred to stop hatred is berserk, only the eternal law of Love can work.

One day this body will die, so ask for forgiveness from all you've made cry.

Pleasures will control all you want, and in your mind they will haunt.

Control desire and you will find, faith, and truth to occupy your mind.

Not worthy of the yellow robe to be, if you lie and desire, and not see.

Full of love, truth, and control, to wear the yellow robe is your role.

Do Good

Wanting all that you don't need, and your root will wither as a bad seed.

Rightfully choosing the correct seed is all in this life you will need.

To be caught up into only fashion, then your mind is given to passion.

With knowledge of passions rule, the mindful will not play the fool.

To suffer and then to do what's wrong, in both worlds you sing a sad song.

Do good and rejoice makes one pure, in this world and in the next for sure.

An evil-doer suffers, this we know, in both worlds this causes woe.

A doer of good delights in this and in both worlds a life of bliss.

Read and recite just to make a sound, ignore living them, and not be found.

Do not sound out words you know, live in them and wisdom will show.

An Island

Conscious of eternal life on earth, paves the way for another birth.

Deny the eternal and life will flee, walking this earth as dead to be.

Wisdom of life is by being aware, to enjoy the wonders of nirvana there.

Meditate and you will find freedom, where nirvana alone is your kingdom.

Glory comes to the one of purity, thoughtful and good this is a surety.

From the Heart wisdom will form an island safe from the storm.

Striving for what pleases the eye so then the soul will surely die.

To learn from the right school, makes one wise and not a fool.

Following after a needless pleasure, causes suffering beyond measure.

Casting away foolishness to be wise lifted up on the mountain to rise.

Mindful

The sage sees the sorrow of the unwise, as his faith is in the powerful sunrise.

Awake and alert the wise will travel, but the others sleep and only babble.

Indra and Joseph both wore the ring, mindful they pleased their King.

Kings and rulers praise the smart fools are despised and told to part.

The monk that is mindful of desire, he grows fast in wisdom as a fire.

Breaking chains that hold them down, conquering fear of sleep all around.

Delighting in the sense of being aware, a monk does fear the mindless snare.

Healthy in mind and soul so well, and so close to nirvana one can tell.

The Arrow

Arrows are straightened to travel a path an unstable mind needs that shaft.

Thoughts flop around like a dry fish, but having a quiet mind is the wish.

No peace with the mind brings, racing around wanting things.

Taming a lion is a goal, easier than the mind that is out of control.

The awaken guard their mind, ever so crafty the wise do find.

Desires can't pierce into this fence, the one made with common sense.

Evil comes to destroy the minds cave, from the heart comes wisdom to save.

Without form the mind will go, control this first and set the row.

Without good teachings to be known, a controlled mind will not be shown.

Focus your mind like an arrow, to follow the straight and narrow.

The Body

An awakened mind is free of fear, no desire to hate for it is clear.

Knowing this body will soon perish, make the mind worthy to cherish.

It's wise to guard against pleasure, not to judge is a goal beyond measure.

What desires can this dead body use when lifeless it can't even muse.

Use your mind and harm another, feel a pain worse than no other.

Doing good with a conscious mind, is greater than a family that's kind.

Flowers

Who will overcome the mighty earth, the one who perfects wisdom's worth.

On this path of wisdom to be, to conquer men and gods you see.

Life in this form is an illusion, desires only create this delusion.

Death is like a flood to carry away the sleeping mind of the day.

Caught in desires of the mind, brings destruction only to find.

Disturbing nothing the sage will, instruct the minds that are still.

Judge the faults of none, only see the good or bad you've done.

Spoken words not lived well, are like a flower with no smell.

A colorful flower smells good, to then live by your words you should.

Garlands are made by many flowers, and good deeds will build tall towers.

Virtue

Even the smell of sweet flowers can't go, against the winds virtue will flow.

Of all the fragrances to compete, virtue is the one that is so sweet.

All fragrances are faint in this debate the gods consider virtue to be great.

Desires never find where they start, ones who walk the path of the heart.

The lotus blooms anywhere it will fall, fragrant and pleasing to us all.

The ones of wisdom will always shine, even with the many in a dark mine.

Foolish

Time on this earth travels slow, to the foolish, who don't know.

Travel the path alone or find, at least one of the same mind.

A fool fears losing sons and wealth, when his mind is in need of health.

One fool thinks he is wise in all and the other is wise to know of his fall.

Wisdom to a fool a Master can't bring, can't even learn a bee will sting.

A moment with a Master one needs to awaken and learn wisdoms deeds.

Fools own enemies are their evil deeds, then having to reap from those seeds.

What a fool does, they will regret, but somehow they always seem to forget.

Seeds

Doing what is good and right, is mindful and will later reap delight.

Deeds done in evil will always grow, in time their sorrow will show.

Deprive yourself is not any proof, follow your heart it knows the truth.

Commit evil and not see the pain, and just like dark clouds it will rain.

Learn all you can to be a master, but neglect to do right, and reap disaster.

Seek recognition in following the way, makes you a fool is what they say.

Control desire and pride then boast, they return and your work is toast.

Live in desire and a world is gained, detachment and nirvana is attained.

Wisdom

A person of wisdom is beyond measure, follow them and find pure treasure.

One that protects you from wrong, evil detests for his will is too strong.

Fools sorrow with the evil and vile, the wise friend the noble and smile

Wisdom is given here in kind, become wise to learn from Buddha's mind.

Fletchers straighten the arrow one way, control your mind seize the day.

A rock is not moved by a storms size, nor does judgement affect the wise.

See the deep lake so clear and still, learn from wisdom and be surreal.

Desires will be back tomorrow, so give no emotions for happiness or sorrow.

Virtue, wisdom and rightness become a song, when the mindful do no wrong.

Wealth, a kingdom, or children ill-gotten, the wise see them all as forgotten.

The Way

Standing on the banks there are more, than the few who cross over the shore.

To live and to learn of the way, all fear even of death has no sway.

Abandon the dark to light the way, delight in nothing and enjoy the day.

Sensual pleasures only cloud the mind, control them, so peace you'll find.

An enlighten mind has acquired this, renouncing things that hinder bliss.

Rejoice for you are rid of strife, for this wisdom brings nirvana to life.

Passion comes with sorrow, break all ties and they're gone tomorrow.

Attachments

The Mindful ones live life like a swan, find a home and then they are gone.

Freedom comes to the wise ones when, desires do not accumulate to begin.

Emptiness is the way to be free, destroy desires and you will be.

Senses wild like horses appear, subdue them so the gods will cheer.

Pure unattached from things they resist, and no longer in this world to exist.

Knowledge is power to gain in size, calm mind, speech and deeds are wise.

Faithless, building karma all for sin, for the mindless they are excellent men.

Inspiring is the place where the one, achieves their Way and is done.

In the forest is without measure, rejoice in the search for no pleasure.

Time

To bring peace by hearing one word, a thousand mindless ones are absurd.

A useful verse makes us calm, but thousands of useless ones set off a bomb.

To recite a verse from the Dhamma, or hundreds that can bring trauma.

Conquer a thousand men in battle, who conquers himself doesn't rattle.

Challenge yourself this way you'll find, not to conquer others just your mind.

Victory and safety, even the gods become mindful you increased those odds.

Sacrifice a thousand days if you will, not worth one without a master still.

Worship, hundred years burning wood, a day of honoring a master could.

One Day

Give gifts for the world to adore, but merit from a master is four times more.

The old and wise bend like a flower, love them and receive gifts to empower.

Better to have one day of peace of mind, than a hundred of being unkind.

Be wise and meditate during this day, not foolish and, joining in the fray.

Live in one day active and alert, than an hundred years careless and inert.

One day seeing things rise and fall, or an hundred years missing their call.

With a master one day there's no doubt, not to live a hundred years without.

Supreme truth seen in one day's time, or an hundred years unseen is a crime.

Drop by Drop

Control your mind, do good quickly if not evil will make it sickly.

To do evil again and again, pleasure turns to sorrow therein.

Do good again and again for in this, finding pleasure filled with bliss.

Sure the evil doer does the deeds and his sorrow grows from those seeds.

Seeds of good take time to manifest, but when they do they are the best!

Think that evil deeds won't come around, drop by drop and then you drown.

Do many good things and don't stop, an ocean of bliss is filled drop by drop.

Evil

Protect our treasures from all that scare and we'll neglect to shun evil's snare.

For the wise one who denies evil's will, so a strong poison can't make them ill.

Fine dust falls back against the wind as evil does the same when fools offend.

The world, heaven or hell all are born again, nowhere the pure of heart begin.

You can run but you can't hide, knowing evil deeds will find where you reside.

Money and gold just can't save you when death comes then you are through.

Aware

Knowing that to die is no thrill, so love each other as self, and do not kill.

See yourself in others so you would, live a prosperous life do only good.

Seeking happiness while you oppress, not going to happen, I will confess.

Try again, but this time being kind, and obtaining happiness you will find.

Cruel words spoken act like a wave, only to return, and hurt like the grave.

When vengeance in you has no appeal, then nirvana becomes more real.

Cowboys drive their cattle to sell and old age drives your life away as well.

A fool does evil and is not aware, and sorrows knowing not from where.

Directions

Violence on the innocent leaves pain and this unwise attempt is only vain.

To offend the peaceful children of a master will bring you a life of disaster.

Living your life causing others pain, you are reborn in hell wishing for rain.

Wear the clothes and to do without, won't obtain purity if mind is in doubt.

The way of a Tathagata there is a plan, so be calm and learn all you can.

Beyond all reproach is to be hip, like the thoroughbred avoiding the whip.

Suffering departs as you learn the way, to reach the other side on that day.

All forms need directions to follow and the way frees the mind from sorrow.

Burn

Peter said the earth is "reserved unto fire", now let your light burn the mire.

Shrouded by darkness is laughter, the earth will burn so what are you after?

Consider letting attachments go, since our body ages and dies, so we know.

A body full of pain and disease, then why hold on to the things that leave?

Colourful autumn leaves are, a sign that all will wither, and die in their time.

This body so full of bones carrying a life, but is also filled with pride, and strife.

Tomorrow

Cars get old and our bodies do too, but doing what's right is ageless and new.

Learn little and only your body will grow, unwise your mind still doesn't know.

To seek knowledge in your lifetime certainly will radiate your on life to shine.

Wisdom now comes to free me, for no longer repeating a life of sorrow to be.

Be young and live like there's no tomorrow, don't grow old and live in sorrow.

Not to obtain wisdom when you're younger, you only grow old, and ponder.

Become

To love yourself you need to be diligent, so in being confident be vigilant.

You will teach others in the way, when "beyond reproach" they will say.

A master lives the life their taught, to live their life in the way is sought.

Find safety in another, this is vain, be your own master it's worth the pain.

Fools do evil so karma leaves them ground as a diamond grinds a gem.

Welfare

Weeds slowly destroy the tree harm comes to the ones filled with depravity.

It's easy to do wrong and to suffer, doing what's good. and helpful is tougher.

Scorn instructions and ignore the rules, a life of sorrow comes to the fools.

Do evil and be defiled or follow the Pure for they are the masters for sure.

Settle this for your own welfare to always help another because you do care.

Radiate

Train the mind to listen to the heart, for this is where wisdom gets its start.

Be awake, not a mindless brother, live well in this world even in the other.

Gain wisdom so you lead a good life, so in both worlds you know no strife.

To see this world with all it's an illusion, death has no power it's a delusion.

Behold this world believes it has power, the truth is, it's a harmless flower.

Being mindless no more, you radiate light in this world from shore to shore.

The Stream

Evil hides the good with a shroud, like the moon it radiates from the cloud.

Darkness in this world only a few can see, they escape from it, then fly free.

Swans follow the sun, flying in the air, masters fly away from desire's snare.

To believe that you have only one life is an evil lie that bring you only strife.

Heaven awaits but not for the miser, happy are the generous that are wiser.

Better than heaven or power on earth is to reach the stream it's more worth.

The Buddha

To be ageless is the term for the way, and so are the masters of their day.

Can you trace the limitless sage who no longer craves the wonders of age?

Buddhas that we hold to be dear, who meditate to be calm and very clear.

In mortal life it's hard to find the truth, a Buddha comes to show the proof.

Learn from the Buddhas to find, doing no evil, only good and peace of mind.

To a Buddha nirvana is their home, but the hurtful on earth they only roam.

Refuge

Living arduously prevents desires, are the teachings the Buddha inspires.

Sensual desires continue on tomorrow, where fine gold still brings sorrow.

Want nothing is a wise man's desire and to limit pleasures takes one higher.

Fear drives men to perches they hide in hills, woods, and even in churches.

Suffering comes from wanting too much, want nothing for it is not a crutch.

Refuge we find in the Buddhas teaching, and the path of fear from reaching.

Harmony

Suffering ends so the way commends, finding peace in wisdom transcends.

The teachings of the Buddha are supreme, and one is released of all suffering.

The wise are not easily found, they are where people prosper all around.

Blessed the Buddha's enunciations are harmony a truth-seekers dedication.

No obstacles are in your path to peace, that's when all sorrows will cease.

Around a Buddha show them respect, who travel a hard road of neglect.

Happy

People are mean, but we are friendly and happy, this is what we bestow.
Hatred is not returned, as we dwell in love, with a free mind to show.

Afflicted the people around us are, the wise find their happiness and live.
Not to give desire a place, the wise are free, and have great love to give.

All the wants desires and greed, we are free from them, and happy to be.
Greedy people are all around, but we are free from that poisoned tree.

Possessions have no control over us, for we live happy in our faith alone.
Like the Gods, they live only on love, and so we shine bright when shown.

Illusion

To compete in life only conjures hate, knowing the loser dwells in pain.
Peaceful they are that don't need to excel to survive who aren't insane.

Out of control the flames of lust will burn and so greed is a crime of living.
Finding peace is one way to nirvana and that will surely start with giving.

The world is full of hungry and hardened people that will suffer with this.
The wise know that it's all an illusion, therefore find nirvana and its bliss.

Being healthy is a gift and to also live in contentment brings much wealth.
A person of trust will be those among friends whom nirvana is not stealth.

Noble Ones

Alone on the mountain, away from pain, the Noble Ones enjoy release.
Undaunted by desires, they know that truth brings deep blissful peace.

Among the Noble Ones there is bliss, and the people are content.
They are very happy when the foolish are not around to lament.

Pretending to run with the foolish only brings you grief and sorrow.
Accompany the wise, to have a happy family, today, and tomorrow.

Follow the noble ones, for they have the qualities that true wisdom brings.
Like the moon follows the stars, these masters will teach only good things.

Detachment

Given to find pleasures in the things of this world, but not in what can be.
Away from those on the path to the stream, these losers will only envy.

Turn away from the loved, and the unloved, there is nothing to gain.
Give love freely to both avoid attachments, for they only bring pain.

Love deeply but hold on loosely, when love's gone it destroys everything.
Not to become dependent on anything leaves a dependency on nothing.

Existence biased on popularity alone will be accompanied by pain and fear.
Competent and alone the wise live free giving no place for sorrow to adhere.

No Place

Rely only on love brings pain and worry, thus the wise are aware.
Free from dependence on love only, they are not caught in a snare.

Attachments do lead to grief and doubts that only grow stronger.
Without attachments the wise don't have these sorrows any longer.

Focus on desires renders a broken heart and a fearful mind.
Being illusion only a master has no place for desires to find.

Material things will not solve your problems of fear and pain.
Send them to the sky, tune into your heart, and use your brain.

Deeds

Honor the ones that embody virtue, insight, and who are always true.
You find them doing what is right, knowing this is just what they do.

Nirvana is beyond words, and to conquer the mind from desires is bliss.
Reaching the stream by mastering oneself, the wise have achieved this.

Like one who, travels far for business, and then returns with much treasure.
So the wise are to their friends, relatives, and to all a very happy pleasure.

Kinsmen welcome their dear ones arrival back with much joy and cheer.
Therefore they are welcomed in the next world by their good deeds here.

Control

Anger leads to hate and pride goes before a fall, so overcome those chains.
Fetters have no place on the master who, is detached, and never complains.

To control rising anger is like taming wild horses and to be their master.
Others who cannot control their anger fail to stop it, as it brings disaster.

Control the angry ones by using peace and the wicked by using good.
Generosity balances the stingy and truth will ruin a liar like it should.

Tell only truths, overcome anger, and listen to your heart then only give.
Do these three things well and be in the presence of where the gods live.

Always

A sage finds restraint over their body from doing harm so they don't offend.
Therefore without reproach, so death has no victory over the sage to defend.

Those being persistent in the mastering of self, they will one day find this.
That as their defilements fade away they will then realize nirvana's bliss.

Know that in this world of illusion we are all blamed no matter what we say.
Blamed when we are silent, speak much or little, and will always be this way.

Always someone is blamed and someone is praised by this world we are in.
Many that are pious do find their power by declaring that we are all in sin.

Earned Praise

Showing wisdom by noticing that day after day the wise will only give praise.
Then these masters have shown true knowledge and virtue in all those days.

Tried by the fires of desire, the wise are blameless, and precious as gold.
Even the gods praise them who have mastered their selves being so bold.

Restraining their body from doing harm is a show of control indeed.
Turning away from harm to sow the good, for this is done by a seed.

The tongue is a weapon that can be used to hurt, be mindful of this.
Do not say words to cause pain, use kindness, and speak only bliss.

The Seeker

Thoughts create reality therefore the seeker banishes anger from their mind.
Not thinking angry thoughts, filling this void with good, and to only be kind.

Practice restraint of bodily harm, in word, and in thought as one should.
Becoming a master of control brings you closer to your stream for good.

Seeing a withered leaf you do know that death is coming and it is surreal.
A life lived not following in the Way, again you will return to this wheel.

Know that to become wise you must make yourself into an island that's sure.
Then empty all impurities, to become a noble one, that's virtuous and pure.

Vigilance

This life has ended, and now with much sorrow, you face the king of death.
Not thinking of tomorrow or to follow in the Way, left you no place to rest.

Become your own master and create an island that's protected from desire.
This is your last body, so you ascend, and another one you will not require.

Master yourself constantly by removing all your impurities to become serene.
Consider yourself to be the silver that the Smith works and then makes clean.

When rust manifests in unkempt iron, the iron will weaken and fall apart.
Evil deeds will make even those who gain sad, and die of a broken heart.

Educate Yourself

Neglect daily instruction for your soul, as the lazy allow their home to fail.
With an ignorant mind you are, like an unclean body that will surely smell.

Lies are a blemish to honesty as stinginess an evil to giving.
To do what's wrong is still evil in both worlds of the living.

Nothing is more evil than ignorance which leaves a mind hollow.
O' Monk educate yourself to avoid the evil that the others follow.

Living is easy for the one that is careless, rude, hateful, and greedy.
Life is harder for the pure, modest, and the one that helps the needy.

Uprooted

Killing, lying, stealing and adultery, numbing their minds by liquor they drink.
Destroying their body, mind and family, they are fools who can't even think.

A good person of wisdom knows that to control evil thoughts is hard indeed.
Masters do not allow greed or wickedness in to plant its sorry evil seed.

Why judge the food and drink that is given by the good will of another?
So your meditation will not be achieved by day or night for this blunder.

Judgment of another's good works uproots yours like a storm does a tree.
Obsessed you are without, where your days and nights are no longer free

.

The Other Way

Hatred's grip on the mindless is secure, for its lust will burn like a fire.
Caught in this net of delusion an endless river of craving they only desire.

Why see another's faults, and not your own, knowing that you have many.
Hide those faults then sift another's, you pretend that you don't have any.

Look for another's faults and then to think this will make you wise?
You are, foolish and only your faults will continue to grow in size.

Not concerned with the eternal, the many delight only in worldliness.
Worrying about the cares of this world, but the wise could care less.

Elder

The wise don't judge without reason, they consider all information given.
Separating truth from lies, judging by the law, that's how they are driven.

Wisdom does not show itself only in words, it's peaceful, friendly, and kind.
Following wisdom by opening their hearts they find peace and a quiet mind.

Old age does not make you a master, without intelligence your life is in vain.
Thoughts mastered by actions of love and kindness, lives lived without pain.

Beauty and smarts don't make one wise, if they envy, are greedy and do lie.
Destroy envy, greed, and lies, live from your heart, and open your third eye.

A Monk

Putting away destructions call by answering hate's request with "never."
The monk doing that will accomplish peace in this life, now, and forever.

A yellow robe does not make the untruthful, and the undisciplined a monk.
Being filled with greed and desire keeps them in a perpetual state of funk.

When evil finds no place to reside in their heart, they are called a monk.
Receiving gifts from others and then not to give back this one is a punk.

Beyond placing a value on material things, this one lives a holy life here.
To understand all opinions of others, truly the monk believes all are dear.

The Sage

Holding in the fool's peace, will only hide their ignorance for so long.
As in holding a scale, the sage weighs all, and then rejects the wrong.

They will be known for rejecting evil and all the desires it unfurls.
Knowledge is a tribute to the sage, who understands both worlds.

You are not noble if you continue to hurt others for no good reason.
They harm no one they are called noble because they are pleasing.

Detachment is not abstaining from life or just spending time in books.
It's the refusal to participate in the world's ways that is full of crooks.

Follow

Find nirvana in the eightfold path, end pain by the four noble truths of life.
Becoming a Buddha and you see why following passions only leads to strife.

Confusing the world with your purity and awareness is but one noble path.
Use of this knowledge will put an end to the suffering of ignorance's wrath.

Truths will manifest the way for the seeker to learn pure detachment here.
All things of this world are evanescent they know this with minds so clear.

Stop chasing after the things that don't last, and see what's of real worth!
Being wise you see that wanting of things only brings sorrow then rebirth!

Pure Mind

A youth's actions unguarded will corrupt the mind and prevent it from trying.
The path to enlightenment will not be found, even though from much crying.

Be mindful of your words, your thoughts, and keep your body from rage.
Control these three monsters and you win the pure path of the great sage.

Quiet your mind to consider directing your thoughts to flow and discern.
Knowledge comes from reflection, ignore this and truths you won't learn.

A man is attracted to a woman because his mind thinks she is like no other.
Then we see him as a young child only wanting the pure love of his mother.

Certain Death

Gently a seeker drops the brief bonds of love, like a flower from a dead hand.
It promotes only the path of harmony to bliss, shown from the one so grand.

Build your home on earth to last forever, to survive heat, snow, and rain.
So you think you can live in this home forever? You are certifiably insane.

The gambler will lose their money, leaving the earnings on the table to bet.
Foolish pride in your wealth will not thwart death not when the time is yet.

Not father, mother, nor family member can protect one from death's rage.
Know this, be wise, meditate, and follow the teachings of the great sage.

Defeat Pain

By sacrificing their attachment to desires the wise then obtain bliss in all.
Finding their bliss can be gained by detachment therefore they won't fall.

The intensity of pain will lead one to live in hatred of others without cause.
But hurting others with their hate will not end pain or even bring a pause.

If fools continue to ignore the warnings of the wise their pains will increase.
They will follow the path of hate and refuse to embrace love's way of peace.

Pain does go away for the ones who are mindful of the body's desire to hurt.
They always choose to do what is right by rejecting wrong and are not curt.

Light Followers

They put to death all illusions of this life in this the wise can be sure.
All wrongs are now forgiven, even murder, and so they become pure.

Followers of Light practice the Buddha's words happily, day, and night.
Always they follow these laws of the universe and with all their might.

The way of Light is to awaken happily, practicing the path of a monk.
Seeing this insight, they will awaken to be mindful of their body's funk.

In living they do not hurt another, these followers of Light practice oneness.
To clear their minds of all clutter, a quiet meditation shrouded in loneliness.

Choices

Detachment in this life is not difficult, if one is not consumed by pleasure.
Then to strive for your home and family only brings troubles to measure.

Run with the pack, you continue the cycle of pain from one life to another.
Follow not after the things of life, free from this illusion you do not suffer.

Reverence is given to ones that are full of faith, purity, and bright as a star.
Their virtues are obtained, and rewards come in their travels, near, and far.

From afar the Pure are noticed, just like a mountain is from many a mile.
The wicked hide and stalk in the night, but in the day they walk and smile.

To be private and uncommitted in life is not for everyone, this is true.
Not to chase after desires, they are happy in the forest, and not blue.

Flames

Liars will be had for they live in denial when caught in a trap of sorrow.
A life of pain caused by deception and after their death the same horror.

Wicked these imposters are, wearing a yellow robe they practice deceit.
Lost they are engulfed in their own flames and then burned by the heat.

To destroy the body by the flames inside would be painful to your health.
But not as painful or as extreme if false monks steal the people's wealth.

There are four penalties given for trying to take another's spouse away.
Loose possessions, insomnia, a bad name, then back again another day.

Outcomes

A disadvantage in this life and in the next will certainly be given.
To anyone that thrives in causing another's marriage to be riven.

As the claymore type of sword has two sharp sides to its blade.
The double minded live a confused life based on their choices made.

One master said "can a corrupt tree bear good fruit?" not on any day.
Then what will the result of your life be, if it is lived in a corrupt way?

Live your life enjoying all that's good, cast no judgements of one, and all.
But to think you are to do nothing, will only open oneself up to a freefall.

Knowing

Doing what is wrong will make you suffer today, and for many days after.
Spending time doing what's good, for this will fill your heart with laughter.

Detachment from desire is worth the building of a wall, this is a good start.
By protecting the wisdom you have gained, for the path of your pure heart.

You are strong and watchful, you hold onto the wisdom from your master.
Not letting desire or want slip into your heart, knowing it leads to disaster.

A confused heart is certainly there when you don't know right from wrong.
Suffering comes by not doing what's right and thinking that you are strong.

Fears Place

Being fearful is not one of the virtues, recognize this emotion, and then know.
That to use it wrongly it will bring you distress, and cause you to live in woe.

Don't ignore what is to be feared, it's more dangerous if you are unaware.
By being ignorant is a life lived in pain, and to be caught in desire's snare.

For the people who call one malicious, but then they don't understand why.
Not seeing how fearful they are who teach, this therefore they should decry.

Learn from the masters and obtain your purity to discern right from wrong.
Living your life pure on this earth without attachments will keep you strong.

Control Yourself

Fearful words, as in anger and hate, are used to hurt, weaken, and deceive.
However the wise who love are pure, and aren't like them who don't believe.

Loud and undisciplined are they, never wanting to learn, they die in the riot.
Learning is the path of wisdom, in the fight the victor is the one who is quiet.

Shortly after their birth the thoroughbred horse is brought up to race fast.
Beyond quiet reflection, as when the going gets rough, the pure will last.

Nirvana is the ultimate inner destination to reach, for there is a path to find.
Don't rely on others to go, because you may only enter by your trained mind.

Ascending Up

Knowledge of nirvana a seeker lives, like an elephant freed from captivity.
They are not interested in the temporary world, but only pure longevity.

Ignorant of the wheel of life, this one does not prosper, slothful in learning.
To grow only in size, not in knowledge, the slacker's wheel is only turning.

The mind is born to wonder wherever desire takes it, but seldom on the path.
Master your mind with wisdom, like a trainer calms the beast without wrath.

In the awareness of your thoughts be glad, rising up as a beast stuck in sand.
Keeping a wise friend you will see that in your troubles they will lend a hand.

Being a Friend

Finding a wise and gentile friend is like finding the needle in a haystack.
You're better off alone so called friends use your soul and then ransack.

Better to be alone, mindful of your thoughts, than among the thoughtless.
Alone to live carefree and pure not trapped in those desires of the careless.

Arduous living blesses all, when needs arise, friends give in love in the way.
Forces of desire subdued by being pure, and to be rewarded in the final day.

The best thing to do in your world is to serve mother, father, friends, and all.
Firm in faith you grow in wisdom, shunning evil being conscious of life's fall.

To Redirect Energy

If you're not satisfied with the blessings you have then confused you'll be.
Going from one pleasure to another just like a monkey swings from a tree.

Without moderation desires will choke, just like the weeds in a garden.
The key to life is to use control, building a foundation that will harden.

Understand the need to redirect the energy of desire into something good.
Therefore it will enable you to break the cycle of being burned like wood.

Desires can be redirected again and again, but they can always sojourn.
Unless no place is left for them to take root, again and again they return.

Direct the path

Desires come in many streams the unwise want them like candy in a store.
The cares of this world pervade their thoughts and drag them to the floor.

Very hard it is to avoid, those pleasures that sweep one away like a flood.
Use wisdom to guide those rivers, like your heart guides the flow of blood.

Desires are all around us, if they are not controlled, as a fire they grow wild.
Overcome by desires one will be unwise and to continue on again as a child.

Chasing pleasures one after another, like a dog circling, and chasing its tail.
Trying only to pursue pleasures instead of wisdom, you create a mental hell.

An Empty Place

Like harmless animals trapped following after things they aren't free to evade.
If we are wise we won't be trapped by pleasures, if we leave no place to raid.

Many give themselves to the life of a seeker, being unfettered from affliction.
Few to find the peace to forever understand, not to return to their addiction.

The wise are aware chains made of metal are not the strongest ones to bind.
To see the control that want of earthly treasures do have on an unwise mind.

Hardening the heart will weigh one down like a stone and cause it to drown.
With no need for hatred the wise see no sense to have those stones around.

Mind is Free

In the web of excessive sensual pleasures, many senselessly are caught.
The wise renounce forms of suffering for in control they've been taught.

Letting go of time, we need to do this before we can cross over life's river.
Becoming timeless when one's mind is free, we therefore do live forever.

Like tightening a rope, evil thoughts will bind one's mind, and never grow.
Chasing after passions closes the mind and captures those that don't know.

Happy they are to reject those evil thoughts, and to meditate on what is right.
Put an end to desires, they only create sorrows, and those who want to fight.

A Tathāgata

Free, the cares of this world are of no concern in the Tathāgata's life.
In full consciousness, they no longer return inside a body full of strife.

Skillful, free in life, and capable they do teach the law of the universe.
A Tathāgata they are all called, they teach those laws, verse by verse.

Gaining knowledge and many things in life, only they, surrender it all.
Clarity of mind, they see inside, their teacher was them who they call.

Finding peace, they are nourished in the teachings of the Buddha they are.
Free to enjoy a conscious mind, they are protected now again by their star.

Peaceful World

Money is not evil, a seeker uses it for good therefore to them it's a tool.
Destroying the unwise, who only chase money, and they act like a fool.

Like the tares to the wheat, lust will destroy them that lay in its casket.
Abandoning desires of lust, the fruit of the wise will fill many a basket.

Live in fear, be like the tares that grow with the wheat, and are then turned.
Choose love as your master, to live peaceful in the world, and not be burned.

Trapped in the illusions of desires, the unwise want the things that fade away.
Free from the desires that delude the mind, the wise are going to profit today.

The Whole Body

See, hear, smell and taste, choose how to enjoy them all to provide a buffer.
Controlling the flesh, the words you say, what you think, you will not suffer.

When the senses are in proper balance, the eye will become silently single.
Being praised by the people, this one will meditate, who does not mingle.

Not drawing attention to their self they are consciously saying little.
Learning words, writings that teach the way to complete life's riddle.

To balance all of one's life on the Dhamma brings a happy heart.
The words bring knowledge to life from them that will never part.

Worry Not

Do not be unthankful for your talents or to worry because others have more.
Be bothered over what others have and your meditation time will be a bore.

They are then content with their talents even though they are very small.
They strive to live a pure life, and are admired by the gods, one, and all.

By not letting the desires of their senses control them, they are made free.
Cares of this world are miniscule, so their inner peace is rooted as a tree.

With knowledge coming from the Dhamma, they will live in pure love.
A Tathāgata's mind is free, and lives in Nirvana, by faith from above.

The Quiet Ones

Unladen with suffering, the Tathāgata's ship sails fast to Nirvana's shore.
They have now conquered all of the five senses, and are to suffer no more.

Be mindful of your thoughts in life, and guard them from excess pleasure.
Be lost in this world of cravings, and you will have pain beyond measure.

Knowing the way does not come to them who don't make themselves aware.
They that are still do awake, and will follow the path to find Nirvana there.

Finding pleasure in their sixth sense, are the quiet ones, who live in the way.
Live your life in the way, only wanting what is needed, to transcend the day.

Becoming Pure

Like the birds of a feather, a seeker will choose to fly with the virtuous one.
Doing this they will not suffer, but living their lives flying towards the sun.

Flowers grow in due season, but when the cold comes their petals will shed.
The seeker grows in time to remove all evil, as they cross over the riverbed.

Peaceful are the ones who master themselves on earth, as they reject greed.
Behind a wall to inspect their senses, they so rejoice, conscious of this need.

Believe in Yourself

When you believe in yourself your heart will feel light, safe, and secure.
Like a trainer that tames lions, the wise ones master their fears for sure.

Having complete faith, and belief, in the wisdom of the way, constitutes bliss.
Therefore the seeker becomes the master of their self, and they achieve this.

The seeker gives themselves to the teachings of the Buddha from their youth.
As a cloudless night reflects light, therefore the Tathāgata's bring pure truth.

Divine

Don't let the things of this world control you walk your path to be divine.
Worldly things pass away, so become mindful to create all that's sublime.

When the divine reach a crossroad in their lives they are not lured astray.
Nor do they worry about the outcomes of a world that only passes away.

Their lives are free from the cares of this world, and are mindful of the way.
Who reach the top by the hard works of letting go, and are happy each day.

Dualities like war and peace, or even night and day, all things live in glory.
The purity of the divine radiate exuberance constantly, writing their story.

A Paradox

Throwing wickedness away, and in its place the outsider will silently aspire.
Deniers they are called, for the outsider has forsaken the weakness of desire.

They may strike the wise one, to look for them to reciprocate you won't find.
A paradox, that would be unacceptable if wrath were to then fill their mind.

Being mindful they don't dwell on desirable things, only something better.
Pain disappears consciously if they hold down their evil wishes like a fetter.

A Buddha has found the restraints through their existence in three ways.
To stop the mind and body from doing wrong, then even words they say.

Pretenders

Comparable to the level of devotion the priest gives to the church's altar.
Seekers show honor to the teacher from whom they learned to not falter.

They become divine, but they do not achieve this through birth or by guise.
By being pure in their lives, the upright are created, and with no surprise.

They try to look the part of the divine, but their hearts are given to desire.
Looks are one thing, but the divine live quiet lives, and purely they aspire.

Birth is just a means of existence, for all are free to be mindful of their walk.
The pure choose detachments, free from desire, so therefore they don't balk.

Heartfelt

Limits are the fears that do paralyze, but a seeker removes those restraints.
Freed from all desires, seekers live their life without any of those complaints.

Wanting creates lies and bitterness of others, from them a seeker will berate.
Their knowledge of the way gives the seeker new skills to therefore separate.

Not being angry, even when harm has come, though they're still in pain.
Quietly controlling their tempers, to master doing this makes them sane.

Heartfelt the upright are, who live constraining their wrath, and desire.
To watch always, being conscious of their bodies, calmness they require.

The Traveler

Water and wind travel, wherever they wish, and can't be seized by hand.
The divine move about, free from pain, unrestricted like the hour of sand.

The wise are not caught in the endless pains of this world that only hurt.
Desires can find no place to dwell, for the mind of wisdom is very alert.

A fork in the road goes in two different directions, know that both are right.
Choosing their path by showing wisdom, the wise reach their greatest height.

Walking on this Earth the traveler has no home, nor any heritage to cling.
Riches or fame hold no abode in their hearts and to breathe air they sing.

Uncommon Ways

Without exception, they who are divine do no harm to any living being.
Nor any action in the taking of a life for to them this is not in unseeing.

Calm if there's a storm, nice to the angry, and serene in the troubled days.
The divine are disconnected from this world and from its burdened ways.

Unable to enter into the divine's mind, therefore vices have no power here.
The boastful will play inside their carnal thoughts, and swindle all who fear.

Words from the divine ones are soothing, healing, and reveal all to be known.
Never cursing others, for that will only undo all that these divine have shown.

Wanting Nothing

To take what is not theirs will only cause many a seeker to slip.
They live their lives in honesty and are safe from passion's grip.

They are free from wanting desirable things that will soon be gone.
The wise do not bring burdens on this journey, nor the one beyond.

The wise don't create places where death can live to cause pain or worry.
With no fear of death in their lives, enjoying each day, they don't hurry.

People need to be praised, but when blame comes they are in so much pain.
Unaffected by needing this, the wise are not concerned, and therefore sane.

Die to Self

Their wholesomeness is a mountain which cannot be moved, even in a storm.
Once they no longer strive for things they can understand their current form.

The river is crossed by the one who has kept themselves from this illusion.
Needing nothing helps the wise find their way, to not to fall for the delusion.

Having a home and a family is the goal of many and few choose to release.
Yet the true disciple will surrender all, to follow the way, and obtain peace.

"He that loseth his life for my sake shall find it." A great master once said.
Therefore finding the path of the way, does not come until desires are dead.

The Other Side

The Divine select to exist in the Spirit world, for there they did before live.
Being in tune with heavenly things, their hearts are open, with love to give.

They have stopped desiring the things that pass away to become very still.
Overcoming any fear of death they quietly remove the stone with their will.

Seeing into the circle of life, they are masters of their body, word, and mind.
No longer clinging to things they are blessed, wise, and relaxed in mankind.

Worthy of Honor

Living without needs a master becomes invisible and leaving no prints behind.
A master's work is unseen, even by the gods, by using the powers of the mind.

Without regarding their past, they have no concern of today or tomorrow.
Nothing burdens the masters, for they are not troubled by pain or sorrow.

Thru quiet meditations they have told the mind to now only follow the heart.
Masters they are, without endless conflicts, steadily they perform their parts

Ready to die they know that their life was an illusion and they know the way.
Seeing their end and their beginning, masters are pure, even the gods will say.